Working in Teams

A Team Member Guidebook

Revised Edition

Sandy Pokras

A Fifty-Minute™ Series Book

Working in Teams

A Team Member Guidebook

Revised Edition

Sandy Pokras

CREDITS:
Senior Editor: **Debbie Woodbury**
Assistant Editor: **Genevieve Del Rosario**
Production Manager: **Judy Petry**
Design: **Nicole Phillips**
Production Artist: **Zach Hooker**
Cartoonist: **Ralph Mapson**

© 1997, 2002 by Viability Group Inc.
Printed in the United States of America by Von Hoffmann Graphics, Inc.

CrispLearning.com

02 03 04   10 9 8 7 6 5 4 3

Library of Congress Catalog Card Number 2001095091
Pokras, Sandy
Working in Teams
ISBN 1-56052-671-8

Learning Objectives For:

WORKING IN TEAMS

The objectives for *Working in Teams, Revised Edition* are listed below. They have been developed to guide you, the reader, to the core issues covered in this book.

THE OBJECTIVES OF THIS BOOK ARE:

❑ 1) To explain what teamwork is all about, what roles you'll play, and how you'll figure out what to do together.

❑ 2) To describe how to make team meetings work, how you can reach agreement with others, and how you can all build your team into a "family" unit.

❑ 3) To present the best ways to follow up on teamwork so others, including the managers who support the whole deal, will listen to your decisions.

ASSESSING YOUR PROGRESS

In addition to the learning objectives, Crisp Learning has developed an **assessment** that covers the fundamental information presented in this book. A 25-item, multiple-choice and true-false questionnaire allows the reader to evaluate his or her comprehension of the subject matter. To buy the assessment and answer key, go to www.CrispLearning.com and search on the book title, or call 1-800-442-7477.

Assessments should not be used in any employee selection process.

About the Author

Sandy Pokras is president of Viability Group Inc., a team-building, communication-training, and management-consulting firm in Northern California since 1973. His training workshops teach team managers, leaders, facilitators, and members to achieve high-performance teamwork.

As a corporate consultant, program designer, keynote speaker, and conference facilitator, Sandy conducts sessions for a wide range of organizations, including IBM, Chevron, Federal Reserve Bank, Westinghouse, the State of Texas, Siemens, University of California, and the U.S. Postal Service.

He is the author of numerous management articles as well as two other Crisp *Fifty-Minute*™ books, *Rapid Team Deployment* and *Team Problem Solving*.

How to Use This Book

This *Fifty-Minute*™ *Series Book* is a unique, user-friendly product. As you read through the material, you will quickly experience the interactive nature of the book. There are numerous exercises, real-world case studies, and examples that invite your opinion, as well as checklists, tips, and concise summaries that reinforce your understanding of the concepts presented.

A Crisp Learning *Fifty-Minute*™ *Book* can be used in a variety of ways. Individual self-study is one of the most common. However, many organizations use *Fifty-Minute* books for pre-study before a classroom training session. Other organizations use the books as a part of a systemwide learning program—supported by video and other media based on the content in the books. Still others work with Crisp Learning to customize the material to meet their specific needs and reflect their culture. Regardless of how it is used, we hope you will join the more than 20 million satisfied learners worldwide who have completed a *Fifty-Minute Book*.

Preface

Welcome Team Members! By joining a team, you have a great opportunity to contribute your energy and ideas to making things work better. It could be great for your development and your career, too. But you might be wondering what teamwork is all about.

The business world keeps changing right before our eyes in so many ways. You were hired because you're good at a specific job or skill. Then all of a sudden someone decides that you and your co-workers should work together in a team. Maybe that was a shock or a rude awakening. It could be difficult if you don't understand how teamwork differs from individual activity.

Webster's dictionary says that a team is *two or more horses harnessed to the same plow.*

Maybe that's why some people get the idea that teams exploit, stress, and squeeze them. However, that's not why modern teams are launched, or how they work.

Why do organizations form teams? Your department might want to get people from different groups together to solve a problem. Maybe the competition is doing better so you need to improve how you do things. Maybe you need to enhance service, delivery time, or quality. Or maybe your manager wants to tap the combined brain power of the whole staff.

Whatever the reason, teams can benefit both the company and you. What's in it for you? You can learn more about your product, service, and business. You can get exposed to other functions in the organization. You can build better working relationships with others. You can get a chance to contribute some of your special talents, and influence how things are done where you work. And all of this can help you get noticed for advancement.

A good team is a group of willing and trained individuals who are:

➤ United around a common goal

➤ Structured to work together

➤ Sharing responsibility for their task

➤ Depending on each other

➤ Empowered to implement consensus decisions

Teamwork doesn't happen automatically. You'll require some input, support, and allowance for growing pains. Your group becomes a team when you get involved, briefed, trained, and prepared, and you accept the challenge.

There are different types of teams. You could be recruited for a period of time to help accomplish a complicated task, solve a problem, improve a work process, or develop a new product. You could be invited to join an existing team with your work group. Whatever kind of team you're on, you will be required to communicate and cooperate.

The revised edition of this book expands upon the basic lessons contained in the first edition, with an updated case study and a new section on virtual teaming to reflect trends in today's workplace. When you and your teammates decide that you're all in it together, you'll start working more closely with each other. If you're also given the power to act on what you decide, you'll know what high-performance teamwork can be.

Sandy Pokras

Contents

Team Nuts & Bolts

Team Direction

Before you commit to a team, you need to know what's expected of you and how your participation will affect your current job. To contribute effectively, you need to see the big picture. What do the customers need? What's the history of the problem? When you first hear about a new team, ask about its mission statement.

Mission Statement: _____

The special assignment, role, or function of the team, usually expressed as a short statement of purpose that defines the scope of the problem, the boundaries of the process, and the needs of the team's customers.

Hopefully the team sponsor, or manager who forms your team, will conduct a team briefing for you and your teammates, explaining the mission, its background, and what's expected of you. When you understand your team's mission and why it was formed, you'll have a better idea of your joint job.

To help you make sense of new concepts like this throughout the book, you'll be following the story of an imaginary team that will go through the steps outlined in this book. Read the first episode on the next page.

Case Study: Software Newsletter Team

Prime Software, Inc., is a company that develops and sells popular programs for microcomputers. Though the software that PSI produces is generally well regarded, Terry, the new marketing director, recently discovered a downturn in customer satisfaction. Apparently Terry's predecessor focused solely on boosting PSI's sales and ignored customer questions and problems.

Terry decided one way to regain customer loyalty would be to revamp the company's customer newsletter. Terry asked Chris, a new programmer at PSI, to join the Software Newsletter Team because Chris's previous employer was recognized in the industry as having superior customer relations.

After reading *Working in Teams,* Chris approached Terry with the question "What's the mission of the Software Newsletter Team?" Terry's rough draft mission statement was:

> *Revamp PSI's software newsletter to focus on helping customers make full use of PSI's programs including tips, tricks, and solutions to real problems.*

Terry talked with Fran, the company's software development director and Chris's boss, who liked the idea. After recruiting a small group of PSI employees and managers to join the Software Newsletter Team, Fran and Terry got everyone together to talk about the idea. Terry's concept and rough mission statement got everyone interested.

Road Maps

Different kinds of teams need different approaches. The road map you choose will tell you the best way to get where you want to go. Following a road map ensures that you don't forget any critical actions. A road map lays out the preferred order of key steps that similar teams have taken to reach their goal. The right road map provides a tested method to guarantee that even first-time teams won't omit essential actions.

With a road map defining in advance the logical order of steps to approaching your assignment, your team can plan and act more quickly. Road maps carve up seemingly overwhelming tasks into more manageable chunks, help you define milestones, suggest tools you can use, and make it easier to hold everyone accountable for results without much stress.

There are seven common road map types, from the simple task to the complex steering council. You will find a brief description of each on the following pages.*

---

*For more in-depth information about specific road maps, read *Rapid Team Deployment* by Sandy Pokras, Crisp Publications.

Road Map Types

Type	Purpose	Key Actions
Task	Implement a well-defined, specific short-term action	1. Contract 2. Plan 3. Do 4. Check 5. Next step 6. Final report
Problem Solving	Eradicate an undesirable, unpredictable, or unworkable situation	1. Organize and plan 2. Describe problem 3. Identify root cause 4. Decide solution 5. Implement corrective action 6. Improve system 7. Wrap up
Process Reengineering	Streamline a working but inefficient process	1. Organize and plan 2. Define requirements 3. Flowchart process 4. Monitor process 5. Make improvements 6. Standardize improvements 7. Wrap up

Type	Purpose	Key Actions
Process Control	Improve results and better control a specific process	1. Organize and plan 2. Define customer satisfaction 3. Describe current process 4. Identify process measurements 5. Measure current process 6. Improve process 7. Assess progress 8. Wrap up
New Product or Process	Develop and introduce a new product or process	1. Organize and plan 2. Formulate a concept 3. Define the requirements 4. Design the new product or process 5. Begin development 6. Initiate testing 7. Implement solutions 8. Maintain product or process support 9. Wrap up

Road Map Types

Type	Purpose	Key Actions
Natural Work Group	Improve a continuing job by working together better	1. Organize and plan 2. Define customer satisfaction 3. Define processes 4. Partner with suppliers 5. Systematize production 6. Measure performance 7. Charter projects 8. Continuously improve
Steering Council	Define direction, establish structure, and coordinate	1. Organize and plan 2. Define direction 3. Initiate data collection 4. Make plans for change 5. Establish structure 6. Define resources 7. Develop a communication system 8. Implement a recognition and reward system 9. Continuously improve

Case Study: The Software Newsletter Team's Road Map

In preparation for an early team meeting, Fran, the team leader, and Terry, the team sponsor, kicked around several proposals for the Software Newsletter Team's road map. Fran proposed the Problem Solving road map to change negative customer attitudes. Terry suggested the New Product or Process road map to clean house and start over. They rejected both because there was already a process in place that just needed improvement. They discussed the Natural Work Group road map, but Terry pointed out that the team may not continue producing the newsletter after its initial revamping. After deliberation, they agreed to propose the Process Reengineering road map to the team since it was applicable to improving the newsletter production process in order to focus on customer satisfaction.

Helping Your Team Succeed

Just because you and your teammates agree to join, success isn't assured. Partly this is because every new group goes through stages. While you're *forming,* you might still be a little cautious, quiet, and tentative. Then as you begin to open up and feel some ownership for what you're trying to accomplish, you'll probably go though *storming.* In this second stage of team development, you'll need to learn to work through differences, tensions, and conflict.

Once you learn to incorporate everyone's input, you'll be *norming,* concentrating on solving problems and making your team activities work more smoothly. Finally, you'll arrive at the *performing* stage where you'll interact so smoothly together you'll be envied for how dynamic, energetic, and productive you all are.

How can you accelerate your growth at these stages to become a high-performance team quickly? Certainly starting with a clear mission and road map, complete membership, and competent leadership are essential. Define what's expected of your team and what power it will have before you get started. Don't rush off and do your own thing until you and your teammates develop some plans and methods to meet, stay in touch, and work in concert.

Focus on speaking up and listening openly so you build trust. Recognize one another's strengths and respect your differences. Aim for synergy, where the sum of all your parts becomes greater than what you could do individually. Above all, make your most important decisions by consensus, where everyone contributes to the group's collective thinking and agrees upon solutions.

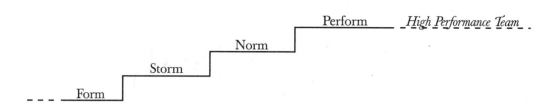

Stages of Team Development

Individual vs. Team Work

Good teamwork depends on working with others and helping them do their part. Cooperation becomes all important. To oil the wheels of a team, you need to understand, get along with, and respect your teammates. Good team members cover for and support each other without being asked. This is a major change for people who've spent their lives being trained to compete, look out for number one, and do things their own way.

Teamwork requires that you get to know your teammates' work histories, skills, and personalities. Plan to visit one another's work areas and to talk about your current jobs. If you pay attention, you'll learn a lot about one another during training and team meetings. You might even have the luxury of a team-building retreat dedicated to building relationships. Spending time and effort building working partnerships will improve team chemistry.

Team chemistry has three parts:

> **Communication**

> **Consensus**

> **Contracting**

We'll discuss aspects of good communication throughout this book, especially when we study supporting teamwork and achieving consensus. Right now we will look at getting closer to your teammates and developing agreements with them, a process we call *contracting*.

Contracting

Teamwork depends on your willingness and commitment. Most people call this buy-in. Developing buy-in means you do important team business by agreement. Agreement forms the basis of any contract.

Contracts: ────────────────

Agreements between team members or supporters to do things for each other, which are binding until renegotiated.

Whether written or verbal, if you don't take your commitments seriously, your team won't work. So think deeply, talk at length, and be open-minded. Remember that any team contract can be renegotiated as needed.

How to Develop Contracts

To develop group contracts, invest the time to talk with your teammates about their needs and wants. Good teams get explicit about what they expect from team members and the organization. You'll make faster progress if everyone listens to and respects others' positions. Team members who take action without others' buy-in aren't very popular. That's why it's important when your team is forming to focus on mission, ground rules, charter, plans, and roles. Your team should first contract among its own members and then get the bosses to contract too.

What types of contracts do you need?

Individual	Group
Your commitment to join the team	The team's mission statement
The roles you agree to play	The team's charter
The ways you'll support your team members	The team's master plan
The tasks you'll undertake for the team	The team's ground rules

Most people commit only when they see a personal benefit in what's required. Combining your commitment with others is a good example of a contract. If you personally value the team assignment, then you're more likely to accept its goals, contribute freely, feel ownership, and support your teammates.

Team Ground Rules

A vital contract for a forming team to negotiate is team ground rules.

Ground Rules: _____

A list of phrases or short sentences that members agree on that define how they want to operate and treat each other.

Ground rules describe things like how you should behave, communicate, prepare for and run meetings, make decisions, solve problems, and resolve conflicts. Good ground rules are clear, consistent, agreed to, reinforced (not enforced or policed), and followed.

As soon as you can, discuss and define the most obvious ground rules. Don't expect to cover every conceivable issue. Just post your initial ideas on a chart that's visible during all meetings. As you run into new situations, add new ground rules, revise existing ones, and drop those that don't fit anymore. Use the questions on the next page as a starting point to establish your team ground rules.

GROUND RULES WORKSHEET

Use the following questions to explore how your team wants to operate. You can distribute these questions for individual consideration and then meet as a team to discuss.

How will we...

1. Work together?

2. Establish plans?

3. Make work assignments and set schedules?

4. Monitor and follow up on work assignments?

5. Keep each other fully informed?

6. Give feedback?

7. Recognize accomplishments?

8. Organize and conduct meetings?

9. Ensure that everyone participates fully?

10. Make decisions?

11. Resolve differences and solve problems?

12. Make the best use of limited resources?

13. Ensure that we achieve desired results?

Organizing

Your Team

Team Support Roles

If you don't figure out what needs to be done and decide who will do what, you'll surely waste time and effort. If each person on a team tries to do everything, the only product will be conflict. So an essential early step for successful teamwork is to define roles.

Several roles are necessary to support cooperation within the team and between the team and the rest of the organization. Following are roles you should define:

Team Sponsor:

The manager who owns the team problem or process, has made the decision to launch the team, and who champions its work.

Typically, sponsors initiate teams by staffing them and authorizing time and resources. They provide direction and guidance, monitor progress, and give timely feedback. They hold teams accountable, promote and support them, and remove barriers. They're the bosses who delegate power to the team to get the job done.

Team Facilitator:

A team process expert who's assigned to help the team with training, team mechanics, and group dynamics.

Since they don't participate in decisions or complete action items, team facilitators aren't full-fledged members. They guide team set-up, provide team training, coach the team leader, and advise the team sponsor on group dynamics, growth, and the handling of problems.

Team Leader: _____

A team member who focuses on building the team and guiding its work or progress.

Team leaders identify goals, communicate action items, and eventually turn over decision making to the team. Team leaders conduct meetings, coordinate teamwork, coach team members, ensure follow-through on plans, and guide outside contacts. Their primary function is to get the team going on the right track before delegating these tasks to the team.

If your assignment is time-critical, management will probably appoint an experienced team leader to get you moving with a shorter learning curve. High-performance teams either let their appointed leaders remain figureheads while they go about their business, or they rotate the function every few months to give everyone some practice.

If you're asked to choose your team leader, think carefully and act wisely. Choose someone who thinks one or more steps ahead, communicates well, and cares about you, your teammates, and your overall work. Don't let this critical decision become a popularity contest.

Case Study: Software Newsletter Team Support Roles

Here's who the Software Newsletter Team appointed to fill the team's support roles:

Team Sponsor. Terry, the new marketing director, had the initial idea for the team and controls the purse strings so naturally filled the role.

Team Leader. Fran, PSI's software development director, was chosen initially because of experience in building other teams. Fran agreed to turn the job over to whomever the team preferred after a few months.

Team Facilitator. Terry asked Ray, PSI's lead trainer, to facilitate the team due to several years of related experience.

Meeting Hats

Though your leader and facilitator may organize and conduct your first few meetings, you'll want to gradually take over these functions yourselves. Most teams distribute these duties to individual team members. We call these unofficial assignments *meeting hats*. Typically, teams rotate these hats occasionally so everyone learns all the jobs needed to make team meetings work. Here's one way to divide up these roles:

Meeting Chair

Calls the meeting to order, reviews the agenda, announces topics and timeframes, and urges the team to stay on schedule. (This is usually the team leader at the outset but can be rotated later.)

Discussion Moderator

Asks questions, introduces discussion tools, keeps conversations on track, and balances participation.

Timekeeper

Asks for timeframes, sets the timer, keeps an eye on the clock, provides time checks, and announces deadlines.

Recorder

Maintains a running summary of everyone's input by documenting and capturing the gist of ideas on a flip chart for public group memory.

Team Member (everyone wears this hat)

Shows up on time fully prepared, speaks up, participates actively, contributes ideas, listens actively, gives feedback, keeps stakeholders informed, reports reactions, aids consensus, and negotiates differences.

If you occasionally rotate meeting hats, you'll take all the power out of one person's hands. By distributing these tasks, you'll learn to take control, include all views, and stay on track. Meeting hats are a great tool to balance communication, build individual responsibility, and share power.

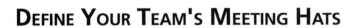

Define Your Team's Meeting Hats

At the beginning of each team meeting, decide who will wear which meeting hat. Together, design a flip chart like this and fill in the blanks:

Meeting Hat	Team Member
Meeting Chair	
Discussion Moderator	
Timekeeper	
Recorder	

Team Member Job Description

As a team member you should be an active player. When you have opinions and feelings about your team, voice your concerns. You tend to be most active when you feel you have a stake in the team's success. For example, your job may depend on the team's success, or your boss may have given you a good incentive to participate. Either way, being a team member includes:

➤ Willingly sharing responsibility for the team's work

➤ Conducting experiments and collecting input before team meetings

➤ Contributing information and expertise during meetings

➤ Representing the team to customers, suppliers, and co-workers

Effective team members are vocal, open, and honest. They listen, support, and cooperate. They stay involved in all aspects of the team's work, and contribute their fair share.

Team Member Job Functions

Support the team:

- ➤ Help define charter, plans, ground rules, and action steps

- ➤ Take responsibilities seriously

- ➤ Cooperate fully with other team members

- ➤ Help resolve team problems

Represent the team:

- ➤ Collect input and gather information about team proposals

- ➤ Keep outsiders informed about team progress

- ➤ Contribute to team reports

Prepare to contribute:

- ➤ Review team meeting minutes

- ➤ Complete actions and follow through on commitments on time

- ➤ Prepare to participate fully and be on time for all meetings

Participate actively in meetings:

- ➤ Think creatively and use brainstorming tools

- ➤ Communicate, listen openly, and help build consensus

- ➤ Recognize others' contributions and encourage feedback

Delegating Team Functions

Most team members realize very quickly that they need each other. Instead of one person doing everything, high-performance teams divide tasks and trust each other to follow through.

A good way to share the load is to create dedicated roles, and refer all similar issues to an internal expert. These mini-leaders guide the whole team in their areas of specialty.

If you need to crunch some numbers, select a team accountant who's good with math. If your project requires technical work, appoint a member with those skills to take the lead. If you have unpopular duties like housekeeping, set up a rotation. Remember, the mini-leader just leads in getting the task done. Everyone should volunteer to assist.

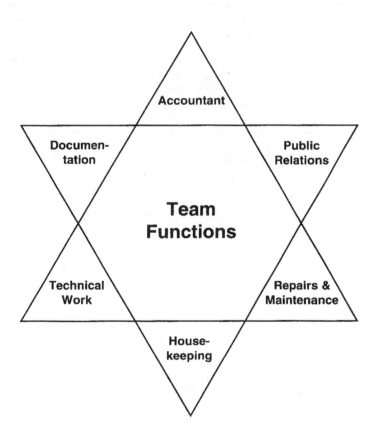

Case Study: Software Newsletter Team Member Roles

Here are the roles and responsibilities the Software Newsletter Team set up:

Team Member	Regular Job Function	Delegated Team Functions
Chris	Programmer	Team minutes
Pat	Technical support rep	Answers to customer questions
Loren	Customer service supervisor	Team accountant
Sal	Technical writer	Newsletter text
Dale	Graphic designer	Newsletter art
Jan	Sales rep	Customer questions & stories

Team Member	Regular Job Function	Team Support Role
Fran	Software development director	Team leader
Terry	Marketing director	Team sponsor
Ray	Lead trainer	Team facilitator

Team Charter

Maybe the most important contract you want to develop as a new team is your team charter.

Team Charter: _____

*A **clearly written description** of the team's mission and how it relates to the organization's goals.*

Your charter should include the authority, resources, and key mechanics necessary to achieve your mission. It serves as the primary contract between members and between the team and its sponsor. A good team charter will:

➤ Give you all the same clear sense of direction

➤ Show you how the team's work fits into the rest of the organization

➤ Help you understand what's expected of you–and what's not

➤ Provide a clear picture of your boundaries and constraints

What Goes in the Team Charter?

Each component of a team charter answers specific questions about the team's direction, membership, and empowerment. We've already looked at several of these components: mission statement, road map, support roles, and delegated functions. Each team's charter is different and may include different components. On the next page are some things to consider as you define your charter.

General Direction:

➤ Background: Why was your team formed?

➤ Mission: What's the team's assignment?

➤ Road map choice: Which generic overall plan should you follow?

➤ Deliverables: What results are expected from your work by what date?

➤ Name: What will you call your team?

Membership:

➤ Customer requirements: What do your customers need to be satisfied?

➤ Stakeholders: Who has a stake in your work?

➤ Team member roles: What functions will core members perform?

➤ Team duties: What group activities will the whole team perform?

➤ Team sponsor role: What does your sponsor commit to do for you?

Empowerment:

➤ Authority level: Which activities can be directly controlled and which need to be approved and how?

➤ Resources: What budget, supplies, training, equipment, and facilities can your team use?

➤ Team metrics: How will you monitor progress and evaluate success?

➤ Reporting: What written and one-on-one reviews and presentations will you make, when and to whom?

➤ Recognition and rewards: How will you be recognized and rewarded for your teamwork?

Case Study: Software Newsletter Team Charter

Most teams don't need to agree on every team charter component at the start of their work, but the Software Newsletter Team did.

General Direction

Background:
PSI's software has long been well regarded by microcomputer users. Recently, Terry, the new marketing director, discovered that there was increasing dissatisfaction among PSI's customers. One cause seemed to be the focus on sales hype in the customer newsletter, driven by the previous marketing director.

Mission:
Revamp PSI's software newsletter to focus on helping customers make full use of PSI's programs including tips, tricks, and solutions to real problems.

Road Map Choice:
Process Reengineering

Deliverables:

➤ A report, within one month, based on customer input, defining requirements for the new newsletter

➤ A new format for the newsletter, within two months

➤ The first issue of new newsletter, within three months

➤ A proposal on how to standardize the new newsletter, within six months, including who should design, produce, and monitor it

Name:
Software Newsletter Team

Membership

Customer Requirements:

➤ Software that works easily at low cost

➤ Quick answers to questions without a lot of hassle

➤ Company response to reported bugs and common problems

➤ A feeling that the company cares first about making its products work before trying to sell customers more

Stakeholders:

➤ Customers

➤ Marketing & Sales

➤ Customer Service

➤ Software Development

➤ Technical Support

➤ Senior management

➤ PSI shareholders and other employees

Team Member Roles:

Team Member	Regular Job Function	Team Support Role
Chris	Programmer	Team minutes
Pat	Technical support rep	Answers to customer questions
Loren	Customer service supervisor	Team accountant
Sal	Technical writer	Newsletter text
Dale	Graphic designer	Newsletter art
Jan	Sales rep	Customer questions and stories

Team Member	Regular Job Function	Team Support Role
Fran	Software development director	Team leader
Terry	Marketing director	Team sponsor
Ray	Lead trainer	Team facilitator

Team Duties:

➤ 1–2 hours weekly: team meeting

➤ 2–5 hours weekly: collect data, meet stakeholders, complete team assignments, and troubleshoot problems

➤ Monthly: informal progress report

➤ As needed: document findings, make presentations, oversee changes

Team Sponsor's Role:
Provide full briefing and access to information, ongoing guidance, timely feedback on proposals, and action on roadblocks. Serve as team champion, troubleshooting conflicting priorities with team members' managers.

Empowerment

Authority Level:

➤ Without requesting team sponsor approval, the team can:

    – Collect data from PSI employees and customers

    – Propose alternate designs and get feedback on them

    – Use PSI marketing resources to produce initial newsletters

    – Manage its own meetings, time, and budget

➤ The team should request team sponsor approval for:

    – Changes that significantly change PSI's public image

    – Modifications to supplier relationships

    – Proposals that promise software features or contain risk

    – Expenditures that exceed the team's budget

Resources:

➤ Time commitment: approximately 10%

➤ Training: Team Kickoff Workshop, team facilitator just-in-time sessions, quarterly retreats, other as needed

➤ Technical support: available through normal channels

➤ Supplies: dedicated network volume, team kit, flip charts

➤ Budget: $17,500

Team Metrics:

➤ Days ahead or behind on team master plan

➤ Team budget

➤ Customer satisfaction index already in use by Marketing

Reporting:

➤ Weekly meeting minutes to team sponsor

➤ Biweekly team sponsor/team leader one-on-one meetings

➤ Monthly team sponsor informal progress presentations

➤ Milestone completion presentations to sponsor and stakeholders

Recognition and Rewards:

➤ Free meal tickets at the end of each step on the road map

➤ $100 bonus for completing major deliverables on time

➤ Team member input to individual performance reviews

You've already read about contracts, so you realize that a team charter is a two-way street. Management has briefed you and has let you figure out the details. You decide what you plan to do, and then your team sponsor approves it. Everyone honors your team charter until you decide to change it.

Treat your team charter as a living document. Review it every now and then, and update it when needed.

Master Plans

The team charter is the umbrella that gives your team a general sense of direction so together you can focus on your assignment. A charter may give you strategy and structure, but before your team can operate like a well-oiled machine, you'll need to decide who will do what and when. Developing team plans together is the tried and true method for smooth high performance. Fortunately, your road map gives you a skeleton to make plan development easier. The following pages will show you how to develop milestones and action plans based on your mission and road map.

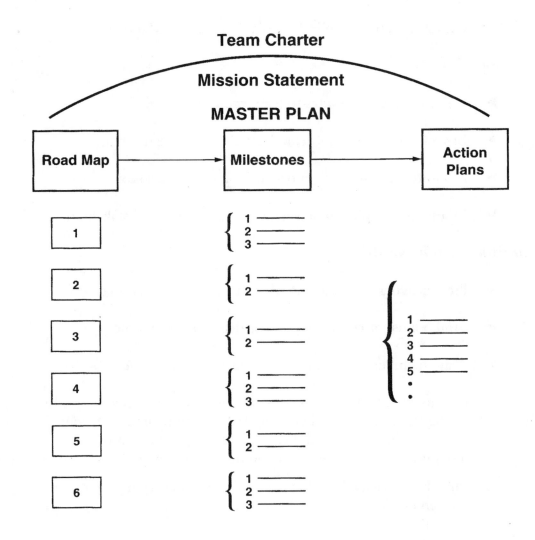

A master plan is an overview of how you and your team intend to achieve results. It includes:

➤ A road map so you can outline the step-by-step route your team will follow

➤ Milestones, the specific, measurable targets your team selects as checkpoints along the way

➤ An overall schedule so you can coordinate efforts and ensure you meet deadlines

Undoubtedly, some member of your team will be familiar with project management software. (If not, recruit someone.) Each program may format your master plan differently, but regardless, the team must develop and agree on the master plan together. Once you've developed your master plan, try to follow it without jumping ahead or getting sidetracked. Do everything possible to stay on course.

How to Develop a Master Plan

Once you've developed a team charter, resist the temptation to jump right into action before completing your master plan. Take some time to brainstorm accomplishments needed for each road map step. When your brainstorming winds down, evaluate what you've listed, collect and combine action items, identify priorities, and select one to three to serve as milestones for each step.

Follow these five steps to develop a master plan.

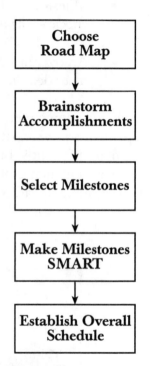

1. Check that the road map suggested fits your team's mission. Adjust it if necessary. If none fits, make up your own.

2. Brainstorm what is needed to accomplish each road map step.

3. Evaluate, combine, and prioritize what you've brainstormed, selecting one to three milestones for each road map step.

4. Make each milestone SMART (**S**pecific, **M**easurable, **A**greed-to, **R**esult-oriented, and **T**ime-bound).

5. Establish an overall schedule by juggling milestone timeframes against the deliverables in your team charter.

Rewrite your plan into one clear document or have your software expert enter the data in a software program. Either way, review the document together before moving forward. Then map out a project-tracking diagram on flip chart paper or via software to document your overall schedule.

Action planning is the continuing sixth step. After the big picture becomes clear, you'll generate action plans. These are the individual steps you and your teammates will need to take to reach each milestone. As you begin working, create action plans to define who will do what by when.

Case Study: Software Newsletter Team Master Plan

Remember the deliverables in the Software Newsletter Team's charter?

➤ A report, within one month, based on customer input, defining requirements for the new newsletter

➤ A new format for the newsletter, within two months

➤ The first issue of new newsletter, within three months

➤ A proposal on how to standardize the new newsletter, within six months, including who should design, produce, and monitor it

Their master plan includes these major results plus smaller milestones arranged around the Process Reengineering road map. Notice they reversed the order of road map steps 4 and 5 to better fit their assignment.

Road Map Steps	Milestones
Organize and Plan	Recruit and train team members this week. Hold first meetings next week to establish roles and ground rules. Agree on team charter within two weeks and master plan in three.
Define Requirements	A report, within one month, based on customer input, defining requirements for the new newsletter.
Flowchart Process	A flowchart, within five weeks, describing the current newsletter production process. A flowchart, within seven weeks, describing the new newsletter production process. A new format for the newsletter, within two months.
Make Improvements	Design first new newsletter together, within 10 weeks. Produce first issue of new newsletter, within three months.
Monitor Process	Design efficient method of canvassing customer reaction, within 14 weeks. Issue report, within 18 weeks, documenting impact of new newsletter.
Standardize Improvements	Adjust newsletter format and content, within five months. Propose how to standardize the new newsletter, within six months, including who should design, produce, and monitor it.
Wrap Up	Decide, within seven months, whether to recharter the team. Hold an awards dinner to celebrate success before team disbands. Review, recognize, and reward team members, within eight months.

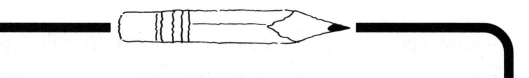

SMART Milestones

Make your milestones SMART using this worksheet.

What do you want the team to achieve?

_____

_____

Specific: What do you want to accomplish?

_____

_____

Measurable: How will you monitor progress?

_____

_____

Agreed-Upon: How will this milestone satisfy each team member's needs?

_____

_____

Result: What is the finished product or final outcome?

_____

_____

Time-Bound: How long will it take to complete this milestone?

_____

_____

Rewrite the milestone to include all the above.

_____

_____

Case Study: Software Newsletter Team SMART Milestone

The Software Newsletter Team reviewed their master plan, and Pat felt the accomplishment, "a new format for the newsletter, within two months," wasn't really SMART. Chris asked how it could be more specific. The team agreed that "format" meant a storyboard and list of specifications.

The team decided that they would measure the quality of the format by comparing each characteristic to the goals stated in the team mission: does it help customers make full use of PSI's programs and offer tips, tricks, and solutions to real problems?

They agreed the action plan would be to review the storyboard and specs with the team sponsor and key stakeholders. The timeframe of two months still worked.

Here is how they rewrote the milestone to be SMART:

> *Present an agreed-upon newsletter storyboard and specifications list to the team sponsor and key stakeholders within two months, demonstrating how each component achieves the team's mission.*

Establish Overall Schedule

Now that you have SMART milestones for each road map step, you need to create an overall schedule. Look at the time required for each accomplishment and the master deadlines in your team charter. Juggle one against the other and adjust milestones to ensure your work will be completed on time.

Action Plans

Consider your charter, road map, and master plan as keys to your strategy, then develop an action plan to define your tactics.

Action Plan: _____

A complete series of steps defining who does what and when in the order necessary to accomplish a milestone.

When you're ready to start a road map step or big milestone, invest some meeting time to figure out what actions are needed and who will be responsible. The best action plans describe who does what, by when, and in what order. Sometimes resources, standards, measurements, or reporting are included as well. Even if you're using software to document and track action plans, team members still need to put their heads together to generate consensus on who will do what when.

Case Study: Software Newsletter Team Action Plan

One of the milestones from the Software Newsletter Team's third road map step was to develop a flowchart, within five weeks, describing the current newsletter production process. Here's the action plan they developed.

Who	What	By When
Sal	Review previous newsletters	May 7
Jan	Interview previous contributors	May 7
Dale	Interview personnel involved in production	May 7
Chris	Draft current production process flowchart	May 11
Loren	Review draft flowchart with those interviewed	May 15
Chris	Adjust flowchart as suggested	May 17
All above	Present flowchart to team	May 20

Team Public Relations

As your team begins to solve problems or improve work processes, you'll probably want to change some procedures. You know that change is hard on some people. That's why an essential part of teamwork is to work closely with people outside the team, relay feedback, and sell them on your proposals.

Stakeholders:

Anyone outside the team who will be affected by the team's work, including internal and external customers and suppliers, co-workers who may appear later in the process, managers who depend on your work output or have veto power, and anyone else whose help you will need or is affected by what you do.

Your team's public relations work starts by identifying your stakeholders. Then you assign them to specific team members whose job it is to stay in touch with them. Group and assign them sensibly. For example, put the sales manager on the team in charge of all contact with sales and marketing stakeholders.

Your team sponsor may be the most important stakeholder on your list. Be sure to review your charter and master plan, once finalized, and regularly forward minutes and updates. Invite your team sponsor to a meeting every month just to be sure nothing is falling through the cracks.

The illustration on the next page shows you and your teammates as the core team. The second ring–consultants–are part-time or occasional contributors who need to be in touch with what the core team is doing. This is also where your team facilitator belongs. The outside ring represents stakeholders, those with whom you will rarely meet, but who have a big stake in your team's accomplishments.

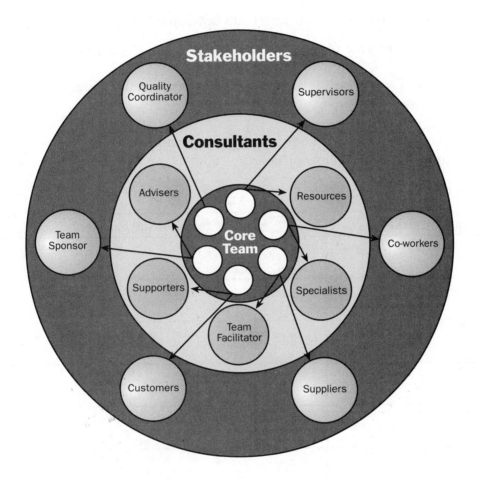

Maintain regular contact and meet individually with anyone you've agreed to represent. Your primary mission is to keep the lines of communication open.

TEAM PUBLIC RELATIONS

Here's an exercise to help your new team develop a PR plan.

1. Brainstorm a list of stakeholders.

2. Analyze what you've listed and organize your stakeholders into discreet groups.

3. Assign one team member to serve as stakeholder rep for each group using the following chart.

Team Member	Stakeholder Rep Role

Working Together

44

Building Your Team

Once you've found common ground by developing ground rules, roles, charters, and plans, you and your teammates should begin to feel comfortable. You're already experiencing the human process of team building as you begin to care about each other and want to succeed together in your joint assignment.

After the forming stage of team building, you and your teammates should:

➤ Know each other enough to build working relationships

➤ Be informed and have discovered your goals and direction

➤ Have a sense of your roles and responsibilities

➤ Have decided to commit to the effort

➤ Be clear that each of you can make a valuable contribution

Teamwork requires that all of you pool information and consider different viewpoints to find solutions and make decisions. Yet, the chances are pretty slim that you'll have exactly the same ideas about an issue. If you let the loudest person make the decisions or just go by majority rule, some members' input will undoubtedly be ignored.

What happens to your motivation when your ideas are immediately rejected? How invested will your teammates feel if their suggestions aren't considered? Expect that contracting will suffer tremendously. Teamwork may totally collapse.

Teams will not bond quickly or solidly without team chemistry. Face it: there's more to teamwork than just facts and figures, charters and plans. Because the human element is vital to your success, you need to routinely make time to work on team building.

Team Dynamics

When your team has developed some common ground, openness, and willingness to work together, you've passed through the *forming* stage. At this point, you may encounter *storming:* tension, friction, and sometimes conflict. Storming is natural. If you take it in stride and learn to adjust to each other, you'll discover that conflict can be constructive. In fact, learning to manage conflict is essential to high performance.

Maybe the best advice for handling storming is to focus on problems not people, on team issues not teammates. That's easier said than done when a teammate criticizes your pet proposal or puts you down. You can learn to handle storming by:

Cultivating Participation:

➤ Let team members talk and be themselves

➤ Encourage everyone to share their feelings

➤ Build mutual trust by allowing each person to vent

➤ Recognize and learn to adjust to different social styles

Resolving Differences:

➤ Identify conflicts as early as possible

➤ Confront and work through differences

➤ Resolve power and other issues as they occur

➤ Always try to negotiate win-win solutions

Negotiating Consensus:

➤ Do your homework, collect data, and canvas stakeholders

➤ Present data you've uncovered and speak your mind succinctly

➤ Ask open questions to discover how to meet teammates' needs

➤ Be willing to listen without judgment

To function well together as a team, you must learn to give each other constructive feedback and to work toward, and reach, consensus. Webster defines consensus as *agreement, especially general opinion.* It comes from the word *consent,* the real issue of teamwork.

When you make a consensus decision, you've agreed to accept, support, and fully act on the decision. Though the selection may not be everyone's first choice, team members should agree that it's workable. You should not out-argue your teammates, get them to give in, and then call it a consensus.

The following pages are all about the tools you need to make consensus decisions: meetings, communication, feedback, brainstorming, analysis, decision-making, conflict resolution, and win-win negotiating.

How to Run Team Meetings

Does this sound familiar? You get a memo to attend a meeting but don't know why. You show up on time and wait around for a few latecomers. Discussion finally starts but time soon runs out. People leave before anything is concluded.

Since teams spend lots of time in meetings, you'll have to improve upon this familiar scenario and find ways to run them effectively. As you're forming, you'll get to know each other, draft ground rules, discuss roles, develop your charter, make a master plan, and meet with your sponsor. As you begin working together, you'll generate action plans, define what data you need to collect and how, review reports from members, and make consensus decisions about your problem or process. And so it goes as you follow your road map.

The bad news about teamwork is that you'll have to meet, meet, meet. The good news is that you can make your meetings efficient and effective with just a few simple tools.

Meeting Agendas

Meetings without agendas are like playing Russian roulette. You might have a great discussion or you might wander off in a frivolous direction. It's best to keep each agenda to one or two major themes to provide better focus in your meetings. Good agendas include a:

Starting time	When you hope to begin discussion on a topic
Presenter	Which member or guest will present or moderate
Topic	A word or phrase that identifies the subject for discussion
Process	The method or tool you'll use to discuss the topic

Use the Software Newsletter Team's meeting agenda on the next page as an example.

Case Study: Software Newsletter Team Meeting Agenda

Start Time	Presenter	Topic	Process
4:00	Fran	*Opening* Call to order, introductions, hats, ice-breaker, minutes, update, agenda	Present and discuss
4:05	Terry	*Body* Senior management meeting report	Present
4:10	Loren	Schedule adjustments	Discuss
4:15	Jan	First improvement plans	Review and approve
4:20	Ray	New tool: cost-benefit analysis	Present
4:40	Sal	Select next improvements	Cost-benefit analysis
4:55	Terry	*Closing* Review mission, plan, and action items; plan next agenda; review meeting	Discuss
5:00	Chair	Adjourn	Consensus

Distribute agendas well in advance so everyone can prepare. Review and be willing to adjust your agenda, if needed, at meeting start.

Group Memory

You might have noticed all the emphasis on writing ideas down on flip charts. Is this really necessary? Yes, it is. To explain why, let's look at how we remember. When you hear or see something, you record it in your individual memory bank. To remember something, you search your personal "database" to find that piece of information, as this diagram shows:

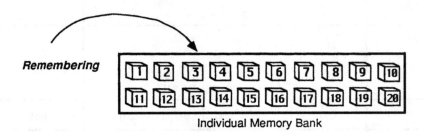

Individual Memory Bank

What happens in a group setting? Experts estimate that we listen at about 25% efficiency. The following picture shows four team members' individual memory banks:

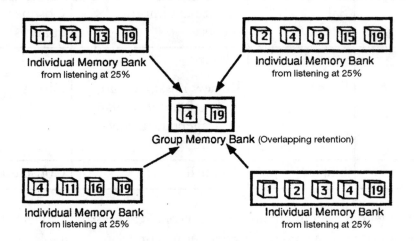

You see, unless a team uses a real-time memory device like a flip chart, they only remember a small part of the discussion. And the part that you remember may be different than what your neighbor recalls. That's why it's important to create a group memory.

Handling Tangents

A meeting tangent is an off-the-point remark that sidetracks a discussion and steers it away from the agenda topic.

New teams can frequently go off on tangents. Instead, you want to develop the ability to stay on topic without wandering off.

Here are a few suggestions to help keep dialogue focused:

➤ Ask if you're not sure what the topic and process is.

➤ Gently remind speakers of the agenda item.

➤ Ask an on-track question to refocus the team on the topic.

➤ Summarize what's been accomplished on the agenda item so far.

➤ Suggest that tangents are captured on a "bin list" for later review.

A good use of flip charts is to capture tangents on a page taped on the wall titled "bin list" or "parking lot." When you hear an off-topic remark, suggest it gets added to the bin. Bin listing is a polite, visible way for you to stimulate open communication while staying on track. By having a public place to capture random thoughts and new insights, you'll encourage each other to think innovatively and at the same time stay focused.*

---

*For more details about running and participating in team meetings, read *Effective Meeting Skills* by Marion E. Haynes, Crisp Publications. Two other valuable books on improving team communication are *Developing Positive Assertiveness* by Sam R. Lloyd and *The Business of Listening* by Diana Bonet, both from Crisp.

Virtual Teaming

The classic picture of a team is a group of athletes on the same field or court, or a group of work associates sitting around a table. In these examples, all the members are in the same physical location.

But the modern world is increasingly becoming a global village. Companies have representatives, manufacturing plants, and customers all over the planet. Problems and processes may have roots and tentacles everywhere an organization does business. Remote employees often feel disenfranchised because they may not be consulted about, or involved in, decisions that affect them.

Which raises these questions: Can you run meetings and build a team with members spread across the country or around the world? Are frequent travel and high expenses necessary to build bridges between members in distant facilities? The answers: Yes, you can build a distributed team with a little extra attention to the tools and mechanics of communication. And, you can build a virtual team relatively inexpensively.

Virtual Team: _____

A group of people in widespread locations with a common purpose and task who use modern technology to connect with each other.

The modern technology a virtual team may use includes cyberspace (e-mail, chat rooms) and conferencing (telephone, video). Since technological means of communication are generally more impersonal than face-to-face contact, consider the suggestions on the next page when building a virtual team.

Team Organizing

Get more input from widely spread stakeholders before you launch a virtual team. Solicit support from decision makers at distant locations. Use extra care when recruiting members. Make distant stakeholders part-time consultants instead of full-time members when appropriate. Do extra preparation to orient and brief the team. Spring for an initial retreat with all members in one location. Make all team charters and plans complete, accurate, and agreed-upon. Ensure time frames are realistic. Consider public relations plans more carefully.

Team Building

Work harder at human dynamics, the most challenging aspect of distributed teamwork. Take differences in culture and language barriers into account. Plan methods that allow long-distance members to get to know each other personally and become familiar with each other's work. Delegate team assignments to pairs or triads of members in distant locations. Regularly devote more meeting time to team building. Encourage frequent e-mail between members. Document and distribute information widely.

Team Operations

Pay strict attention to team mechanics. Consider time zone differences. Make sure that meeting agendas and minutes are timely. Have meeting chairs follow agendas and time frames. Teach and encourage discussion moderators to call members by name, conduct frequent verbal check-ins, poll for reactions, and balance participation. Ensure consensus is fully supported by all members. Use input and technology to ensure that all members participate fully in team presentations.

Monitoring Progress

Have team leaders check in with distant members often. Keep team records, action registers, and project plans and documents accurate and accessible. Encourage more member-to-member feedback. Amplify team member reinforcement. Act more swiftly to troubleshoot delays and problems. Ensure accountability with more mid-course contacts. Be more scrupulous with stakeholder public relations contacts and team self-monitoring.

Supporting the Virtual Team

Did you notice that these tips urge you to follow the tools and guidelines in this book carefully? The crush to meet deadlines and get things done can often undermine team mechanics. With a virtual team it is even more imperative that you don't let this happen.

To ensure critical team tools and dynamics function effectively, here are some tips for those playing team support roles.

Team Sponsor

Do your homework when recruiting and briefing the team. Ensure team charters and plans meet your expectations. Stay in close touch with team operations. Regularly touch base with members in distant locations.

Team Leader

Be vigilant about team building and conflict resolution. Be sure meetings are well planned and well run. Coach members on assignments between meetings. Follow up scrupulously on all action items.

Team Facilitator

Be extra attentive that the team sponsor, the team leader, and team members know their roles. Watch team dynamics carefully. Provide creative and workable consensus-building tools.

Team Communication

One of the most important ingredients of successful teamwork is effective communication.

Effective Communication: _____

An interchange of ideas and feelings resulting in mutual understanding.

Would you rather work with teammates who are arguing or communicating? When you're arguing, your goal is to win the competition by forcefully selling your proposition. When you're communicating, your goal is to understand everyone's viewpoint.

Good communication depends on clear speaking and active listening. To stimulate dialogue and encourage others to listen, be **assertive**. State your ideas positively and declare your position with confidence. Say what's on your mind, give reasons for your opinions, and suggest improvements. Don't argue and turn off your teammates. Instead speak up, give specific facts, and stay focused. Be open, direct, expressive, and genuine. Show that you can remain objective.

Presenting your views isn't enough, though. You've got to **listen** effectively, too. Concentrate on trying to understand your teammates' thoughts and feelings. Focus on a wide range of communication hints—body language, emotions, vocal tone, and your own intuition—to consciously absorb your teammates' messages. Signal acknowledgment when you understand, and ask questions when you don't. Summarize and give feedback so that you're an active, not a passive, listener.

TEAM COMMUNICATION GUIDELINES

Here's a table that summarizes points to keep in mind to effect good team communication:

DO	DON'T
Be organized • Focus on desired results • Have an agenda • Crystallize ideas before speaking • Complete communication cycles	Don't be disorganized • Be unclear about your purpose • Wander around • Speak before you think • Introduce tangents
Be assertive • Be clear and use specifics • Level with others • Get to the point • Give constructive advice	Don't be aggressive • Blow smoke with generalities • Hide your concerns • Beat around the bush • Find fault
Listen actively • Concentrate with empathy • Be interested in others' views • Notice body language • Check if others are finished	Don't block others • Keep thoughts to yourself • Object to others' views • Avoid eye contact • Interrupt

DO	DON'T
Be open-minded • Welcome feedback • Be comfortable with controversy • Allow venting • Give feedback	Don't be closed-minded • Avoid confronting issues • Get emotional • React to others' reactions • Suppress your feelings
Respond • Acknowledge statements • Clarify • Summarize • Offer solutions	Don't resist • Counter with your views • Assume • Argue • Blame others
Dialogue • Ask open questions • Ask directly for straight answers • Alternate speaking and listening • Look for common ground	Don't be one-sided • Answer your own questions • Ignore answers • Dominate the conversation • Find fault with your teammates

The bottom line of team communication is dialogue. You all need to balance speaking and listening. Ask each other a lot of questions and encourage everyone to explain his or her reasoning. Give feedback after hearing each other out. Combine what you hear with your own ideas. Look for agreements and suggest solutions everyone can accept.

TEAM COMMUNICATION

Use the following table to assess how well your new teammates communicate. Rate each item using a 1 through 10 scale with 1 being the lowest, 10 the highest.

Tool	Application	Rating
Listening	Concentrating	
	Duplicating the speaker's intent	
	Reading body language	
Presenting	Giving specific information	
	Amplifying statements	
	Proposing solutions	
Questioning	Asking for information	
	Asking for clarification	
	Asking for agreement	
Responding	Giving clarification	
	Giving feedback	
	Building on others' input	
	One-word acknowledgment	
Summarizing	Playback	
	Paraphrasing	

Feedback

Feedback means one teammate's reaction to another's actions or statements. Healthy teams learn to communicate their reactions quickly and constructively. They negotiate until everyone is happy, and then hold each other accountable for the agreements made.

Teams still in the *forming* stage typically do not give much feedback, especially when things go wrong. Let's say, for example, you agree on ground rules, plans, or action items. Something unexpected gets in the way and you aren't able to follow through as promised. Because you're still forming, little is brought up in public. But you can bet some members are grousing to each other in private.

When you reach the *storming* stage, your team will open up more, even if things are still a bit unharmonious. For example, if you miss an action item, you'll hear about it. This is progress.

In the beginning, you may want your leader or facilitator to give all the feedback. While this helps bring short-term comfort, it's better for all of you to struggle with the learning process. When you have the confidence to handle whatever comes up, storming will be a distant, nonthreatening memory.

When to Give Feedback

You might find yourself giving feedback in situations when teammates:

➤ Don't seem to understand

➤ Bring up brilliant ideas

➤ Take discussions off track

➤ Show attitudes that make you comfortable or uncomfortable

➤ Change for the better

➤ Use language you object to

➤ Violate some ground rules or disrupt the team

➤ Do things that are helpful to you or the team

➤ Aren't opening up because authority figures are present

➤ Dominate discussions or grandstand when the team isn't interested

Notice feedback can be positive or negative. Sometimes feedback works better one-on-one and sometimes it works better with the whole group. An example of one-on-one feedback would be telling a teammate privately that a meeting was a waste because he didn't complete an action item. An example of whole-team feedback would be pointing out that many team members are late with action items. Then the group can deal with the bigger issue together.

One-On-One Feedback

Let's look in more detail at the two kinds of one-on-one feedback recommended for teamwork: positive reinforcement and advice. Researchers estimate that most children receive 35 times more negative feedback than positive while growing up. To counteract this conditioning, teams should use 80% reinforcement and only 20% advice. This works because if you give positive advice too often, people just hear negative criticism. You positively reinforce by acknowledging, encouraging, and praising at every opportunity, and agreeing and siding with your teammates when you agree.

POSITIVE REINFORCEMENT GUIDELINES

Here are some suggestions about how to give positive reinforcement:

Encouragement Your purpose is to encourage a specific action, behavior, or performance so that it will be repeated.

Pure Mixing reinforcement with criticism or advice dilutes it and may poison the desired effect.

Positive Your aim is to reinforce what you want, so concentrate on the positive and ignore undesirable actions.

Value Expressing the value of the person's actions must genuinely acknowledge them to be effective.

Support Your feedback should support what people are trying to accomplish or what they are having difficulty with.

Specific Action Recognize a specific event or behavior because general compliments tend to be taken as empty praise.

Descriptive Your feedback should describe in detail what worked, what you liked, and why it was good.

Understandable What you say should be clear, without unfamiliar technical terms or buzzwords.

Genuine Use genuine statements, not canned phrases the same way over and over, or your sincerity will be questioned.

Immediate Try to catch people doing something right, because reinforcement is strongest within 30 minutes after action.

Frequent Use positive feedback following each performance until the behavior is routine.

Reduce Later Once your recognition is accepted, gradually reduce the amount you give so teammates don't become dependent.

ADVICE GUIDELINES

Even if you use all of the reinforcement techniques suggested, you will still need to adjust and improve things. But remember, advice should only constitute 20% of your feedback.

Here are some similar guidelines about how to give teammates advice:

Receptivity   Make sure your teammate is ready and willing to receive advice.

Descriptive   Your feedback should describe in detail how things are being done and how you think they should be changed.

Results   Back up your advice with proven results, actual reports, testimonials, or statistics.

Suggestions   Whenever possible, couch your advice as a suggestion, not as a must or a should.

Manageable Chunk   Give only a small amount of advice on one subject at a time.

Balance   Mixing advice with encouragement or compliments sometimes reinforces that you're honestly trying to help.

Positive   Ensure that you show that you really believe that your advice will help the person and team improve.

Tone   Keep your tone friendly and upbeat and avoid using a critical attitude or talking down to the person.

Just-In-Time   Give your advice just before the action is to occur so your teammate can practice right away.

Feedback   Ask for comments and reaction at any time to allow for clarification and keep communication open.

How to Accept Feedback

Just because you use constructive feedback doesn't mean that advice like this is easy to accept. Here are some ideas about how to accept advice. Using these techniques yourself when you are offered advice will demonstrate positive behaviors to others and will show that you are open to feedback.

➤ Listen carefully and try to see things from the other's point of view

➤ Breathe deeply and stay calm

➤ Clarify using questions to make sure you understand

➤ Acknowledge what you hear and understand without arguing

➤ Sort out what you've heard and decide what you agree with

Respond only after you've completed the above steps.

Team Feedback

The easiest way to give advice is in private. Often, this is the best way for people to hear things and agree to change. But ultimately, teams need to be up-front with their feedback in a group setting. To be effective, team feedback must be constructive, specific, and ongoing.

DO	DON'T
Be constructive	Be destructive
Help each other learn and grow	Bash or put each other down
Suggest actions to take	Gang up on an individual or idea
Be fair	Be negative
Be objective and impartial	Whine and complain
Be honest	Be judgmental
Be assertive and get your point across	Disguise criticism in off-the-wall comments
Convey practical observations	Convey blanket generalities
Be specific	Filter your comments
Give concrete, meaningful details	Have a hidden agenda
Provide supporting examples	Be reluctant or hold back
Be consistent	Spring surprises
Communicate openly	Indulge in knee-jerk reactions
Give interim feedback	Overreact

REINFORCEMENT PLANS

Place a checkmark (✔) by any methods below that you plan to use:

❑ A friendly, smiling, interested attitude

❑ Catching someone doing something right

❑ Expressing confidence in a teammate's ability

❑ Frequent one-word acknowledgments like good, right, or fine

❑ Verbal praise when someone solves a problem

❑ Personal compliments about a teammate's strengths

❑ Compliments for asking good questions

❑ Concerned questions to find out how a person is doing

❑ Accepting your teammate's input and suggestions

Consensus Decision-Making

The reason you'll invest lots of time and effort in conducting meetings, collecting data, interviewing stakeholders, presenting your findings, and giving constructive feedback is to eventually make sound consensus decisions.*

Team Consensus: _____

A decision or position that reflects the collective thinking of a team and that all team members participate in developing and actively supporting.

Since unanimous decisions are rare, most team consensus is an idea that merges the best thinking of all team members. Sometimes one suggestion is accepted as universally best, but most often the team's position combines individual thoughts.

How to Reach Consensus

To reach consensus, all team members must:

➤ Express themselves clearly and participate fully

➤ Be open-minded, listen fully, and respect others' views

➤ Respond verbally with acknowledgment and feedback

➤ Propose solutions to differences and be willing to negotiate

➤ Identify areas of natural agreement and actively seek consensus

---

*For in-depth coverage of this topic, read *Achieving Consensus* by Eileen Flanigan and Jon Scott, Crisp Publications.

Face disagreements and explore solutions until you find a win-win. Everyone must feel that their viewpoint has been heard and that they have contributed to the collective outcome.

How can you make this work quickly and effectively? The diamond diagram below shows the three phases of communication that you need to move through to make a consensus decision. First, you generate ideas by stimulating discussion, using open questions, and brainstorming creatively. The top of the diamond shows that you're trying to pry open minds at this point.

When you record all input on charts for everyone to see, analysis becomes easier. Get everyone to understand others' ideas by reviewing what's on the charts. Then chart or evaluate all the input. The challenge in the middle of the diamond is to turn the corner toward a conclusion instead of wandering off on tangents.

Finally, make a consensus decision by summarizing, eliminating, and narrowing. When you've narrowed down your objectives into a small list, then you can figure out how to include the remaining items through ranking, prioritizing, and formulating win-win proposals. The bottom of the diamond shows that you've arrived at one point of agreement.

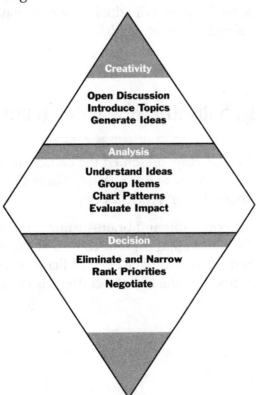

Creativity

Open Discussion
Introduce Topics
Generate Ideas

Analysis

Understand Ideas
Group Items
Chart Patterns
Evaluate Impact

Decision

Eliminate and Narrow
Rank Priorities
Negotiate

When to Use Consensus Decision-Making

Many teams use the consensus process exclusively once they've mastered it. This decision-making approach is open and fair, but it's also demanding, time-consuming, and often requires skilled facilitation, especially at the beginning.

You'll certainly want to use consensus for important decisions such as:

➤ Your team charter and master plan

➤ The ground rules you'll follow

➤ Decisions with major impact during the course of a project

➤ Final analysis of a problem

➤ Resolution of a team conflict

➤ Commitment to a course of action when collective action is needed

If you're deliberating on minor details, don't use consensus decision-making. Take a majority vote, leave it up to individual choice, or have the team leader decide. Don't consensus your team to death.

Case Study: Software Newsletter Team Decision

To begin, the team facilitator, Ray, presented the consensus diamond and briefly explained some of the tools to use at each phase. Then, Fran took over as meeting chair and led them through the process.

As a result of lots of data collection and brainstorming, the Software Newsletter Team came up with a list of 33 ideas on how to format the new newsletter. Obviously, adopting them all would have been difficult and confusing. So they needed a structured method like the one the consensus diamond offers.

Consensus-Building Tools

Each phase of the diamond has its own set of tools. Team tools don't look like saws, hammers, and drills. They're specific discussion methods, ways to chart ideas, or techniques to compare opinions. Flip charts, bin lists, and road maps are examples.

Once you've played with all of them, you can choose the ones that best fit your situation. Until then, rely on your team facilitator—helping you choose the right consensus-building tool is a facilitator's specialty.

Creativity Tools

The first stage of building consensus is applying creativity to stimulate discussion, build participation, generate ideas, and brainstorm lists. You want to suspend your judgment about what you're working on. The consensus diamond suggests three sets of tools for the creativity phase:

Open Discussion

Begin conversations by checking in with members and using unregulated conversation to quickly surface reactions.

Introduce Topics

Introduce topics by systematically starting conversations and clearly defining the discussion tool that the team will use.

Generate Ideas

Moderate discussions by asking open-ended questions to build participation and stimulate creative thinking. Get team members to brainstorm ideas and build on each other's comments without editing or judging.

To master the creative stage, teams need to become skilled in brainstorming.

Brainstorming

Brainstorming is *an idea generation tool in which members of a group toss out in rapid fashion whatever answers come to mind in response to a key question, build on each other's ideas, and compile a comprehensive list of everyone's ideas at the end.*

The best way to make this tool work effectively for your team is to follow these guidelines.

Clear Question

Clearly announce the focus of the brainstorming session. Post the exact question on a flip chart.

Suggest Ideas

Contribute whatever ideas come to mind, striving for quantity, not quality. Cover all wild and crazy viewpoints.

Accept Everything

Accept all ideas, however impractical or unorthodox. Listen and acknowledge. Post all contributions using the speaker's words. Use multiple recorders if needed to keep up.

No Editing

Don't edit, criticize, or evaluate any suggestion. Discussing ideas isn't brainstorming! You'll have time to clarify later.

Build On

Let comments trigger new thoughts. If you react to an idea, volunteer different ones instead of judging or editing.

BRAINSTORMING TOOLS

There are many ways to generate a flurry of creative ideas during brainstorming. Here are some favorite team tools:

Card Deck   Each member writes separate ideas on cards or slips of paper which are combined in a deck and discussed by the whole group.

Post-it®   Each member writes their ideas on individual Post-its which are stuck to the wall or flip chart in full view of everyone.

Round Robin   One member shares an idea with the group verbally, then the next person shares an idea, and so on. The discussion continues round and round in an orderly fashion until everyone has passed.

Bouncing Ball   One member catches the ball and volunteers an idea, then throws the ball to another person who volunteers an idea, and so on.

Popcorn   In any order, individuals spontaneously throw out one-word or short-phrase answers which summarize their position on an issue.

Free Wheel   All team members spontaneously share ideas at will with the whole group, with others building on their ideas.

Case Study: Software Newsletter Team Creativity

Ray suggested the team use Post-it® brainstorming to quickly surface the range of ideas in members' minds. Fran as meeting chair called the meeting to order. Loren, serving as discussion moderator, suggested the brainstorming question. Twenty ideas on individual Post-its were stuck to the wall within the first few minutes. Loren asked the team to look at the items and decide if everything they had considered was posted. More Post-its went up. After a little more prompting, the team decided the list was complete—for the moment—at 33.

Brainstorming Question: *What format do we want for the revamped software newsletter?*

Newspaper format

Grass roots input without management oversight

Simple and easy to read

Fast turnaround answers to questions

Valuable information

Lots of little tips and tricks

Colorful

Include different industries

Answers to questions

Slick glossy magazine

Stories from other users

Not dominated by Fortune 500 customers

E-mail format

Include the little guy

Available on the company's Web site

Small pages with one topic per page

One newsletter per program

Multiple topics per page

Each newsletter covers multiple programs

Short articles

Written by users

Long in-depth articles on very specific program features

Technically accurate

Some newsy chatty light-hearted stories

Making PSI look good

Announcements of new programs

Not strongly sales oriented

Advance warning of new versions and features

Encourage future purchases subtly

Survey questions asking for input and feedback from customers

Wide variety of content

Letter-sized format folded in envelope

Lots of graphics

It was clear from the wide scope of the list that every member had a different idea of what format meant and some had conflicting opinions. But that's the nature of brainstorming—you accept whatever comes up and work with it.

Analysis Tools

Once you've thoroughly discussed a topic, make sure that everyone clarifies, understands, and values all ideas. Truly hearing each other is typically the greatest challenge in consensus building. Sometimes inexperienced teams don't document all opinions. Some team members may try to force a decision before everyone has contributed his or her thoughts and feelings.

The analysis phase prevents this scenario from getting out of hand. You'll find the tools for analysis below, organized in groups having to do with *understanding, grouping, charting,* and *evaluating.*

Understand Ideas

There are four ways to better understand what you've brainstormed. They all focus on getting each of you to carefully consider each other's ideas. Wise teams almost always use at least one of these tools after brainstorming.

Silent Reflection	Quietly read over your lists so you personally think about everyone else's ideas.
Clarification	Identify unclear ideas and then get the original contributors to explain their intent.
Amplification	Ask contributors to go into more detail or have other team members build on each concept.
Buzz Groups	Split up into pairs or subgroups to discuss the ideas on the list and then report what you discussed to the whole team.

Group Items

Once everyone says they've fully digested everything on the flip charts, you can reorganize similar ideas into sets. Grouping isn't always the best next step, but if you can predict it will be, plan to brainstorm with Post-its® that can be easily rearranged.

Affinity Grouping	Move similar items into groups, using Post-its or item numbers, and name the sets.
Combination	Identify similar ideas and combine their wording to make composite items.
Categorizing	Identify common themes on the list, name these categories, and then label each item.
Outlining	Organize items into headings and subheadings with items and subitems.

Chart Patterns

Charting, an alternative to grouping, results in a picture, graph, or visual display. It takes a bit more effort than simple grouping, but sometimes it's worth the trouble to clearly show important relationships between your ideas.

Mind Mapping	Graphically draw relationships between items on a chart to show visual connections.
Cause-Effect	Post items in categories on a cause-effect diagram to show causal relationships.
Pareto Chart	Post data on a stacked bar chart that shows how often an event occurs or how much impact it has.

Evaluate Impact

You can also evaluate the impact or relative value of your ideas. Some of these tools border on decision-making. Use them to compare items so that you're ready to narrow, prioritize, and decide during the next phase.*

Impact Analysis	Number items and then list the consequences of each idea, one by one, on a separate chart.
Pros and Cons	Define the advantages and disadvantages of each item, one at a time, using a two-column chart.
Cost-Benefit Analysis	Discuss potential costs and benefits or risks and rewards of items to identify relative value.
Forcefield Analysis	Discuss how to minimize and maximize forces driving and restraining a change.

*For more information on these analysis tools, read *Facilitation Skills for Team Leaders* by Donald Hackett and Charles L. Martin, and *Team Problem Solving* by Sandy Pokras, both by Crisp Publications.

Case Study: Software Newsletter Team Analysis

To begin analysis, Ray suggested the team silently review the list of 33 ideas for a couple minutes before clarifying. Fran suggested that the discussion moderator check for full understanding by asking if any ideas needed clarification. After a few moments discussion on several items, everyone seemed clear on what everything meant. Adjustments were made to flip chart entries.

Next, Fran suggested that the team break into buzz groups of three for a few minutes of open discussion to identify how much agreement they had about what was on the list. Five minutes convinced the group to invest more time on this overall subject. Here are their flip chart notes capturing individual comments:

Brainstorming Question: *How much agreement do we have on the format of the new newsletter?*

➤ Some agreement

➤ Agree on customer focus

➤ Many different definitions of format

➤ What about technical questions?

➤ What about software bugs?

➤ Widely varying format proposals

➤ Don't ignore programmer input

➤ Not much agreement

Next, Ray suggested categorization. They chose the following categories, which turned out to cover everything:

F = Format layout

C = Contents

L = Look & feel

D = Delivery

S = Standards

Then the team discussed which category each item fell under and labeled them as follows:

F   Newspaper format

S   Grass roots input without management oversight

S   Simple and easy to read

D   Fast turnaround answers to questions

S   Valuable information

C   Lots of little tips and tricks

L   Colorful

C   Include different industries

C   Answers to questions

L,F Slick glossy magazine

C   Stories from other users

S   Not dominated by Fortune 500 customers

F,D E-mail format

C   Include the little guy

F,D Available on the company's Web site

F   Small pages with one topic per page

C   One newsletter per program

F   Multiple topics per page

C   Each newsletter covers multiple programs

C   Short articles

L   Written by users

C   Long in-depth articles on very specific program features

S   Technically accurate

C   Some newsy chatty light-hearted stories

S   Making PSI look good

C   Announcements of new programs

S   Not strongly sales oriented

C   Advance warning of new versions and features

S   Encourage future purchases subtly

S   Survey questions asking for input and feedback from customers

C   Wide variety of content

F   Letter-sized format folded in envelope

L   Lots of graphics

After labeling all items (with the discussion moderator's guidance), Jan asked what they had accomplished. A brief open discussion revealed that they better understood the options everyone had in mind, but the team still hadn't reached a consensus decision about format.

Decision Tools

Most struggling teams complain that their greatest weakness is difficulty in arriving at consensus quickly and easily. In most cases, this trouble can be traced back to little merging of good ideas. This, of course, depends on creativity, flip charting, and analysis. Yet, even good preparation doesn't guarantee a consensus decision, much less a good one. Decision tools fall under the categories of *narrowing, ranking,* and *negotiating.*

Narrowing Tools

Your list might have already narrowed while understanding, grouping, charting, or evaluating. If it hasn't, get it down to a manageable size for decision-making using one of these elimination and narrowing tools.

Elimination	Use specific criteria or intuition to remove items that obviously seem impractical or unworkable to everyone.
Multivoting	Ask members to vote as many times or for as many items as they want by raising fingers as the discussion moderator reads down the list or by posting adhesive dots on the charts. By voting for several items or voting several times for your top item, you'll weight priorities to help weed out weak items.
Straw Polling	On each item, ask for a show of hands or thumbs up/ sideways/down to determine which ideas to retain and which to discard.

Warning: If you use these narrowing tools for final decision-making, you can easily exclude minority views. Use them to determine team member leanings, not to blindly accept the numbers to avoid conflict.

Ranking Tools

Next, you will probably want to use one of these tools to rank priorities.

Discussion Ranking	Use open discussion to quickly sort best to worst. Switch to another method if progress is too slow.
Individual Ranking	Using individual ballots or a public scoring chart, post each member's ranked items from best to worst and then add up the scores. Always use high numbers for the top rank so that winning items score highest. When it would take too long to completely rank a long list, simply use a 3, 2, 1 scale.
Pair Comparison	Compare the top two items on the list and reverse the order if the second one ranks higher. Then compare each subsequent pair the same way. Work up and down the list until each item is in proper relation to each other.
Sequencing	Arrange the items on the list in order of sequence: which should be done first, next, and last.
Decision Matrix	Use a matrix to rank items in columns using different criteria. Rank by ballot or discussion. Establish final priorities by adding each of the scores from each ranking.

Just because you've prioritized doesn't mean you've reached consensus. Look at the results of any tool, take a moment's open discussion to check what you've learned, and see if a decision is imminent.

Negotiating Tools

If you haven't stumbled into complete agreement as yet, use one of these tools to combine the most important ideas and negotiate proposals.

Grouping Tools	Use grouping tools to categorize items or combine the best ideas into a proposal everyone can support.
Trial Balloons	Focus attention on proposing alternatives to bridge the gap between opposing points of view.
Win-Win Solutions	Ask team members to come up with new ideas that merge existing options into solutions that satisfy everyone.

Case Study: Software Newsletter Team Decision

To get closer to a decision about newsletter format, Fran suggested the team first eliminate any listed suggestions that weren't strictly format ideas. In a moment it was clear to everyone that they needed to get consensus on the items categorized F for format layout, which spanned contradictory proposals. Pat suggested that items labeled D (delivery), C (content), and L (look & feel), would be easier to negotiate if they built a solid consensus around the F list. Dale suggested that items labeled S for standards should come first, even before deciding about format. Without realizing it, the team had used the sequencing tool to organize their decision process. With everyone's agreement, Fran moderated a round robin, checking reaction to the list of standards. Everyone easily accepted everything on that list.

Ray suggested checking for any other format ideas before moving forward. Sal added a new idea to the list, "mail and e-mail one-page one-topic announcements." Ray next taught the team to do multivoting using adhesive dots, issuing three dots to each team member, about one-third as many as the eight items on the format list. Ray suggested each member distribute their dots on their three favorite formats, or put two or three dots on ones they felt really strongly about. Here were the tabulated results:

Question: *What format do we recommend for the Software Newsletter?*

O   Newspaper format

1   Slick glossy magazine

3   Small pages with one topic per page

4   Multiple topics per page

1   Letter-sized format folded in envelope

5   E-mail format

2   Posted on the company's Web site

2   One-page one-topic announcements sent via mail and e-mail

When reviewing the results of multivoting, the team agreed to drop the items with one or no votes. It was obvious e-mail was a popular format, but there still appeared to be a controversy about how many topics should appear on each page.

Fran then asked if anyone had any suggestions on how to decide. Loren proposed a trial balloon, thinking that they could design a format which included all the popular ideas. Ray suggested breaking into buzz groups of two to see who could design a win-win solution incorporating all of the format ideas into one unified plan. Chris and Sal suggested a medium-sized page format with some pages going into depth and other pages covering smaller tidbits. Everyone enthusiastically endorsed the brilliant consensus, which fused the best thinking of all team members and left no one feeling that their views were dismissed.

Handling Differences

Being human, team members are naturally different. Many teams are purposely recruited with built-in differences in the hope that team members will work them out and eventually use them to their advantage. As a result, tension within teams is expected. Most gradually overcome these frictions and become productive. But if team members focus solely on "What's in it for me?" or "What's wrong with her?" instead of "What's in it for the team?" progress gets slowed down.

Conflicts are critical forks in a team's path. Maturing teams learn how to work through or around personal needs without undermining the team. This often stimulates creativity and opens stagnant minds. On the other hand, inexperienced teams sometimes make things worse by ignoring situations until they blow up. They may label those who speak up as "non-team players" and treat them as second-class citizens, which turns conflicts personal. Don't sweep recurring tensions under the rug. Talk to your team leader about them sooner rather than later.

The following flowchart shows how poorly handled differences turn into disruptions. If the team doesn't handle the disruptions according to the previous feedback guidelines, conflict can result.

Differences

The natural diversity of the people who make up the team and the unique functions they represent

➤ Backgrounds, education, and upbringing

➤ Values, beliefs, and philosophies

➤ Personal styles and preferences

➤ Job priorities and department objectives

➤ Individual ambitions

Disruptions

People feel friction and discomfort: the team gets distracted, wastes time, and gets off track

➤ Action items not completed

➤ Ground rules not being followed

➤ Domination, deference, and little cooperation

➤ Unwillingness to share workload

➤ Criticism and negative feedback

Conflict

Complete communication breakdown with emotions out of control

➤ Built-up tensions finally explode

➤ Nonstop venting and dramatizing

➤ Meetings out of control

➤ Team members quit or don't show up

➤ Permanent damage to relationships

Conflict Resolution Principles

The techniques in this book can help you understand others, work around disruptions, and avoid arriving at a full-blown conflict. Roles, ground rules, charters, plans, communication, feedback, and meeting agendas are just a few of the tools that prevent differences from escalating into disruptions and worse, blowups. You sure don't want to fall into a complete communication breakdown with flaring tempers. But if you find your team slipping, follow these principles to deal with it:

Step 1: Welcome Differences

➤ Find something positive in every divergent view

➤ Incorporate all statements into team discussion

➤ Document all comments on flip charts

➤ Recognize, don't avoid, frustrated team members

Step 2: React Positively

➤ Create a safe place for team members to air differences

➤ Keep a positive attitude in the face of conflict

➤ Demonstrate belief in teamwork by being constructive

➤ Patiently but assertively moderate discussion, and allow venting

Step 3: Use Empathy

➤ Listen visibly, actively, and as an ally

➤ Ensure everyone feels that their voice is heard

➤ Consciously focus on the ideas and feelings of others

➤ Try to see things from others' points of view

Step 4: Use Positive Feedback

➤ Use recognition and advice and "I" statements

➤ Focus on the situation, not the person

➤ Coach by being direct, specific, assertive, firm, and helpful

➤ Use accepting body language to show clearly that others count

➤ Balance everything you do with sincere positive reinforcement

Step 5: Confront Problems

➤ Explore differences by discussing all sides openly

➤ Find root causes, not symptoms, to find permanent solutions

➤ Take personal responsibility whether it's your problem or not

➤ Turn all conflict situations into learning opportunities

Step 6: Negotiate Solutions Together

➤ Negotiate win-win using collaboration

➤ Use ground rules to find joint answers

➤ Use the team's creativity to brainstorm alternatives

➤ Facilitate group decision-making by seeking consensus

➤ Build ownership by letting the team solve its own problems

We've already seen that step six, negotiating solutions together, is a powerful decision tool. It's the crux of digging your way out of immobilizing team conflicts.

Case Study: Software Newsletter Team Conflict Resolution

The Software Newsletter Team fortunately arrived at a consensus format decision. But along the way, they ran into heated opposition between Dale, the graphic designer, and Pat, the technical support rep. After it became clear during the previous process that they were miles apart, Ray intervened and guided them through the six steps of conflict resolution.

Step 1: Welcome Differences

Loren, the discussion moderator, guided the recorder to note Dale's and Pat's statements on separate flip chart pages. The team helped capture simple phrases that represented their views. Dale was strongly in favor of larger, colorful, diverse pages with graphics and multiple topics per page. Pat was vehement about answering burning user questions without glossing over the details for the sake of art.

Step 2: React Positively

Loren asked other teammates what they agreed with in Dale's and Pat's ideas. In turn, Dale and Pat were asked to amplify their views and back them up. Their ideas and the team's positive reactions were added to the flip charts. Everyone experienced some relief of tension by looking at the positive.

Step 3: Use Empathy

At Ray's suggestion, Loren asked Dale and Pat, one at a time, to explain each other's posted views. With some coaxing and prodding, they each restated what they'd heard.

Step 4: Use Positive Feedback

At Ray's suggestion, Loren asked Dale and Pat, one at a time, to find something they agreed with in each other's posted views. Oddly enough, when focused on the positive, they each saw the value in each other's concerns.

Step 5: Confront Problems

Loren asked other teammates to give their view of Dale's and Pat's conflicting views. Everyone agreed that, due to past history, both issues were valid: the new newsletter had to be user-friendly and appeal to customers, and answer their questions. Dale and Pat really lightened up hearing that everyone accepted both their positions.

Step 6: Negotiate Solutions Together

When asked what would satisfy each concern, Chris jumped in asking the team why the new newsletter couldn't have some pages with lots of graphics and art, and others focused on one technical topic. Sal amplified the idea until everyone agreed in principle.

Win-Win Negotiating

The only negotiating style that works effectively in a team is win-win. That means that what makes you happy should also work for those on the other side. You need to focus more on common interests than on personal gains. You're looking for solutions to joint problems and lasting agreements that all of you will take seriously. You need to agree instead of argue, cooperate instead of compete, and solve each other's problems instead of selfishly looking out for number one. If you succeed in negotiating a win-win solution out of a conflict situation, you'll increase commitment, reduce bad feelings, and prevent long-term grudges.

Here are four win-win methods with desired actions to replace competitive or contrary bargaining:

Method	Do	Don't
Build Working Relationships	• Seek common ground • Separate people from problems	• Search for weakness • Look for advantages • Attack opponents
Explore Options for Mutual Gain	• Openly lay out needs • Share information	• Bargain, haggle, and horsetrade • Make concessions
Satisfy Both Sets of Interests	• Consider objective merits • Base decisions on principle	• Employ leverage • Base actions on manipulation
Solve Each Other's Problems	• Use wide-open creative thinking	• Limit thinking, dig in, close your mind • Use ultimatums

P A R T 4

Monitoring

Progress

Monitoring Team Progress

Whether your team is working on a project or a continuing job, you still need to manage your work jointly. Project management really means to follow up on your plans, monitor your progress, reinforce what's working, and troubleshoot what isn't. If you don't, someone above you will and you could lose whatever empowerment you started with. That's one reason why you must spend time on charters and plans at the very beginning. Then you've already decided what to monitor and how to follow up and you've contracted for sponsor support.

Monitoring is best done by the whole team continuously so that you stay in touch with your position on your plans and schedules. Use monitoring to check team chemistry, remind each other what needs to be done, and set up early warnings. It's better to find out early that your plans need adjustment. Frequent fine-tuning averts crises. By checking routinely, you might also discover what support members need to finish their work.

The three Ps of project management remind you to monitor:

➤ **P**lans, such as charter deliverables, master plan milestones, and action plan assignments, to know if you're ahead of, behind, or on schedule

➤ **P**rocesses, so you're continuously observing how well you're working together, what tools you're using, and how your dynamics are changing

➤ **P**ublic relations, to make sure you pay special attention to how well your communications are working with customers, suppliers, and stakeholders

Monitor all three routinely and you'll always know where you are and how to make quick adjustments.*

---

*For more information, read *Project Management* by Marion E. Haynes, Crisp Publications.

Good Monitoring

The best monitoring is simple, reliable, accurate, and an integral part of the work itself. That way it won't take special effort to stay up-to-date. Here are a few monitoring methods to choose from.

Project management software	A software program that documents deliverables, milestones, actions, resources, and timeframes, and tracks progress
Project board	A timeline diagram that shows major milestones with start and finish targets
Presentation and review	Team members, satellite teams, or the whole team formally present status and answer questions
Regular activity reports	Written progress reports distributed weekly or monthly
Action plan review	Team walk-through of the status of action assignments on the plan to complete one milestone
Production statistics	Regularly collecting, distributing, posting, and analyzing data about production volume and quality
Common drive	A networked folder, volume, or hard drive containing all team documents accessible to all team members
Budget controls	Regularly collecting, distributing, posting, and analyzing financial data
Work sampling	Conducting quality control spot checks
Operator checksheets	Forms that operators use to record data about routine actions, events, and critical incidents
Dummy run	Walk through or role play an existing procedure, new process, or action plan to see how it's working
Checklist evaluation and audit	Reviewing a standard list of actions or questions to determine how well things are functioning
Customer satisfaction surveys	Identifying customer perception using written questionnaires or telephone polls
Customer focus group or interview	Getting feedback from outsiders through one-on-one or group discussions about team progress

Project Management

The essence of monitoring teamwork is project management, which has six steps. Start with measurable plans, keep clear records, self-monitor your team's health, respond to what you find, conduct presentations as needed, and wrap up properly. Easy, right? Well, maybe not, but at least easy to explain.

1. Measurable Plans

You already know that to track progress you need to:

➤ Follow the right road map for your kind of work

➤ Develop a master plan with a few milestones for each road map step

➤ Document your master plan on paper or in project software

➤ Post your master plan on a flip chart at each meeting for a visible reminder

➤ Break each milestone down into small measurable steps with an action plan

➤ Review your master and action plan status at the end of each meeting

➤ Update your planning documents or software immediately following each meeting

2. Recordkeeping

Recordkeeping isn't the most popular team duty. But without it, monitoring suffers. To get support and implement solutions, you need documentation. Team recordkeeping includes:

➤ Transcribing activities and decisions into official team records

➤ Maintaining agendas, minutes, plans, statistics, and reports

➤ Posting plans and documents on team public network volumes

➤ Creating reference materials for team findings

Keeping records will help you focus, keep outsiders informed, confirm commitments, provide reminders, and create a historical database. Two tools are essential: action items and meeting minutes.

Action Items: _____

Tasks that team members agree to complete by a specified time.

It's easy to lose track of team activities in the midst of a busy work schedule. Your solution is to track assignments so that you don't forget your responsibilities and commitments. That's why an action item list may be the most important written record you'll ever use.

Action items record who agreed to do what by when. Action items are identical to steps of action plans except they come up spontaneously during meetings. To ensure that action items are completed, your minutes secretary should distribute the list within 24 hours after each meeting. Don't bury the items in the back of your minutes. Instead, put them at the top of the front page.

Case Study: Software Newsletter Team Action Items

Here's the list that the Software Newsletter Team issued after a meeting in the middle of their third road map step.

What	Who	When
Publish report of customer feedback.	Chris	June 7
Collect stakeholder reaction to report from team members.	Sal	June 27
Plan team meeting to decide which adjustments to incorporate in newsletter design.	Fran	July 1
Prepare mock-up of second newsletter and distribute before next team meeting.	Dale	July 10
Document recommendation to team about continuing customer feedback.	Loren	July 15

Distributing action item lists after each team meeting is a great idea, but by itself doesn't guarantee that things will get done on time. If you don't review your actions at each team meeting, some may be forgotten. And as you can see from the Software Newsletter Team's list, some assignments take longer to complete than the time between team meetings. Will anyone remember action items from three meetings ago?

Action Item Register: _____

A perpetual listing of action items which a team adds to, keeps track of, and checks off when assignments are completed.

To maintain an action item register, simply split the *when* column into *date due* and *date complete* columns. Your project management software may include this feature or you may just want to create a simple spreadsheet document in this format:

What	Who	Due Date	Date Complete

Instead of issuing a separate action item list after each meeting, add new items to the action register and include a copy with meeting minutes. Review the entire list at each meeting, date those that are done, and adjust target dates or other action items as needed.

Meeting Minutes:_____

Meeting minutes are the journal of team activities. Good minutes are brief, well-organized, readable, self-explanatory, accurate, and distributed immediately.

They help you record your findings, recall your reasoning, reconstruct your thinking, report your problems, and recognize your progress. They take time to compile and read, but they save time and effort by keeping outsiders and missing members up-to-date.

Meeting minutes should include:

➤ Date and time of meeting plus team members attending

➤ Major agenda items with any key conclusions or decisions

➤ Action items or action register

➤ Date and time of the next meeting, and any known agenda items

If you feel the need to elaborate, you could include:

➤ Reports of action taken between meetings

➤ Discussion summaries for each agenda item

➤ Key data or stakeholder input reported

➤ Informational attachments distributed at the meeting

➤ Mission statement and road map and master plan position

Just make sure that you don't go overboard. You want to make generating minutes as easy as possible.

3. Team Self-Monitoring

Though documentation is necessary for project management, paperwork alone won't ensure your team's progress. To grow quickly through the stages of group development, you'll want to invest a little time in monitoring your team's health by:

➤ Tracking how well you're working together

➤ Raising your awareness of team dynamics

➤ Learning which team tools work and which don't

➤ Adjusting and refining team ground rules

If you occasionally spend a little time talking about how you're doing, how you're feeling, and how you could do better, you'll improve continuously. Feedback from trainers, facilitators, and other experts is helpful, but if you also give each other feedback, you'll progress faster. That's how high-performance teams take charge of their own growth and find their emerging team identity.

So establish checkpoints, solicit open feedback, analyze your performance, and routinely assess changes in your dynamics.

Some self-monitoring techniques include:

➤ Reviewing the meeting process each time you adjourn

➤ Receiving feedback from your team facilitator

➤ Analyzing meeting minutes for signs of group dynamics

➤ Holding team retreats and troubleshooting meetings

➤ Having one-on-one discussions outside the meetings

➤ Conducting peer performance feedback sessions

➤ Regularly using group process checks

Group Process Check Method

In addition to being a great way for team members to guide their own growth, group process checks (GPC) are a diplomatic way for leaders or facilitators to guide team progress without being bossy. Especially when emotions are rising, someone has to exert a firm, calm hand to defuse tensions. Otherwise inexperienced teams could do permanent damage to some members' self-esteem.

Group Process Check: ─────────────────

An intentional time-out called to focus team attention on how well the current group process is working.

You can use this simple six-step procedure to call a GPC:

Awareness	A team member or team facilitator observes how a group process or ground rule is working and its effect on your team.
Time-Out	The observer decides the situation warrants change or recognition and calls a group process check by giving the agreed-upon time-out signal ("GPC" or "time-out").
Feedback	The observer quickly explains what was observed with neutral and factual feedback.
Process Review	The discussion moderator holds a brief "here and now" meeting so that you can all quickly assess the issue with a moment's open discussion.
Response	If appropriate, you can all suggest solutions and select the best alternative to deal with the situation. You might want to adjust or add to your team ground rules at this point.
Return	Quickly, the discussion moderator should direct you back to the last point of the previous process before the GPC.

Meeting Review

Meeting reviews are a simple and powerful self-monitoring tool. You just need the discipline to take a couple of minutes at the end of each meeting to check in. You can each fill out a form or use open discussion to determine thoughts and feelings.

The simplest and quickest method is the "Plus-Delta Chart." Use popcorn brainstorming to get team members to throw out words or phrases summarizing what worked well and post them in the "plus" column. Then do the same for the "delta" column, asking what should be changed or done differently next time. (Don't brainstorm what's wrong; always ask for what would work better.)

+ Plus	Δ Delta
What worked well?	What would work better?

For a written review, have everyone fill out a simple form like this:

Meeting Review	Poor				Great
How well did our agenda work?	1	2	3	4	5
How well did we manage time?	1	2	3	4	5
Did everyone participate?	1	2	3	4	5
How open was our discussion?	1	2	3	4	5
How good was our pace?	1	2	3	4	5
Did we get closure on desired results?	1	2	3	4	5

Someone will need to compile the scores so you can discuss the summary at the next meeting.

4. Respond

Keeping records and monitoring both progress and process aren't much good unless you respond to what you find out. Like any other feedback tool, you have two main actions: supporting and troubleshooting.

Support each other by encouraging teammates. Remember to use positive reinforcement. A team of cheerleaders has more fun and accomplishes more than a team of sharpshooters and undertakers.

For example, when you hear good news from stakeholders, pass it on. When a teammate handles something well or solves a problem, make a big deal out of a public announcement. When you've completed an action plan, reached a milestone, or finished a road map step, celebrate. And when someone needs a hand, volunteer. When you find a teammate with less experience than you in a particular job, coach him or her. You'll probably get twice the same support back later when you really need it.

Troubleshoot quickly when monitoring uncovers actual problems. If your early warning system is working, clues will surface about potential troubles before teamwork grinds to a halt. That's the time to stop and take a look. Maybe you'll want to hold a special team meeting to analyze where you got off track, brainstorm solutions, and adjust your plans as needed.

For example, treat overdue tasks as problems, investigate what's causing the delay, find solutions, and work around the obstacles. Suggest that team members discuss barriers to project work with their bosses or recruit your team sponsor to help. If you find upset customers, bring them in to a team meeting, calm them down, find out what's bothering them, and decide what you can do to satisfy their needs.

Troubleshooting Tool

Just because you run into an unexpected obstacle in the middle of a project, you shouldn't change your master plan. You might need a short detour, but you don't need to switch to the detailed team problem-solving road map from the planning chapter. To work through a small obstacle, a temporary resource gap, a minor personality conflict, or an unexpected change, you need a narrower approach.

The troubleshooting tool is a quicker and simpler alternative for this situation. Use these four key problem-solving steps in order.

Problem Description	Discuss facts and perceptions until you identify the central issue and agree on a label that defines how things differ from how you want them to be.
Root Cause Analysis	Analyze what's causing the problem until you identify the most fundamental reason the situation hasn't been resolved.
Solution Decision	Brainstorm strategies to resolve the root cause until you agree on a solution.
Implementation Plans	Develop an action plan to put the solution into action.

Case Study: Software Newsletter Team Troubleshooting

After printing the first new, expanded, colorful newsletter, the Marketing Department's print shop e-mailed Terry saying they couldn't produce future versions on the Software Newsletter Team's proposed schedule. Here's the troubleshooting summary the team attached to their next minutes:

Problem Description	We need high-quality, high-volume, quick-turnaround printing for the new newsletter. The Marketing Department's print shop can't commit to our schedule. We can't lower our standards or wait for them and still achieve our mission of producing an in-house revamped publication.
Cause Analysis	The print shop has multiple demands on their facilities by many stakeholders, many of which are seasonal. Budget doesn't exist to go to an outside vendor. In retrospect, the team realized the print shop's needs and situation were never taken into account. After some research it was discovered that the newsletter printing schedule coincides with several peak demand periods for the shop.
Solution Decision	By shifting three nonessential publication dates, software newsletter printing could be scheduled for low-demand print shop times. Gerry, the shop manager, agreed to commit to support the team if constant communication was assured.
Implementation Plans	Gerry agreed to join the team as a part-time printing consultant. The team agreed to consult regularly with Gerry about proposed size, format, and volume changes for the newsletter. Terry was elated by the deal.

5. Team Presentations

To ensure that your solutions are understood, adjusted, and supported, you need to get skilled at giving interim reports to stakeholders. To get your decisions approved, you must make convincing formal presentations. If you want your improvements to stick, you need to conduct group training sessions.

Possible Situations	Possible Audiences
Negotiating direction and plans	Team sponsor
Asking for resources and support	Management team
Collecting data and getting feedback	Customers
Summarizing progress at key milestones	Suppliers
Solving obstacles in the team's way	Other employees
Training others on findings	Industry/community groups
Making final reports	All the above stakeholders

Presentation Preparation

A good presentation has four elements:

➤ An opening that warms up the audience

➤ A purpose

➤ A body of material

➤ A conclusion

Use these steps each time you need to present.*

1. Decide the ideal result you want from the presentation and formulate a statement of purpose to explain it.

2. Brainstorm topics and anticipate audience questions and put them in order to build an agenda.

3. Decide on timeframes for each agenda item.

4. Decide who will present each point or lead each discussion. Be sure you involve as many team members as possible so you demonstrate consensus.

5. Prepare written agendas, visuals, graphs, handouts, or written reports that will help get your points across and involve the audience.

6. Plan how to involve the audience with introductions, an opening warm-up, and questions to stimulate feedback.

7. Arrive early, set up the room, and rehearse if time permits.

*For more information about developing your presentation skills, read *Effective Presentation Skills* by Steve Mandel, Crisp Publications.

Completed Staff Work

Many teams are dissatisfied with the amount of power and authority they have. But often the team sponsor isn't completely up-to-date. So why isn't informing the boss more of a priority?

When you update your boss, you create another problem. You've given a busy manager another issue to research, another battle to fight, and another decision to make. Ever heard the phrase "putting a monkey on the boss's back?" Making work for your sponsor can slow down the decision process. How can you take the initiative to solve problems independently?

Proposal and Report

The best method is a Completed Staff Work (CSW) proposal. A CSW is a report that documents your thorough analysis of a situation and a presentation of your proposed strategy. It quickly shows that you've done your research and you understand the problem and know how to fix it. In addition, a CSW document and presentation show the alternatives you considered, why you think your solution will work, and how you will implement it.

If the CSW is complete and accurate, the team sponsor doesn't need to start over, launch an investigation, or dream up other options. Since everything is defined, all that's needed is a quick read, a succinct hearing, and ideally, rapid agreement. At least your team sponsor can explain how you can gain quick approval. All of this work dramatically increases your chances of getting to yes.

CSW CONTENTS

CSWs provide a brief review, sponsor confidence, and quick decisions.

Overview   Subject and purpose of document, simple problem label, summary conclusions, your recommendation.

Situation analysis   Description of the situation and need, key facts that define the problem, current data that explains any effects of the problem, relation to organization goals, and a clear statement of the problem's root cause or most basic need.

Recommendation   Clear statement of your proposed solution or decision, why it's the best strategy, benefits to gain, and costs or risks of implementing this recommendation. Include the other options considered and why you rejected them.

Implementation   Action plan to implement the decision, proposed budget and financial analysis, clear statement of what the reader needs to do, what will happen next if approved, and space for the manager's decision and comments.

Keep your CSW to a page or two for quick reading and presentation. It's better to attach backup documentation rather than clutter the proposal itself. Any documents that need to be reviewed before a decision, or issued afterwards, should follow. Include reports, spreadsheets, charts, announcement memos, purchase orders, or other vital documents.

6. Project Wrap-Up

How often have you found yourself reinventing the wheel? To prevent that from happening to others, you need to document and present what your team did, right and wrong. Yes, this takes time and effort. But it's worth it so others can go forward without wandering around in a wilderness that's already been mapped.

Your first wrap-up task is to develop a final report that documents the team's course of action and accomplishments. Compare what you planned with what you did, and objectively evaluate how the team fared. Your report should describe your entire project from beginning to end. Place a checkmark (✔) in each box as you complete and include the item.

- ❏ A brief summary

- ❏ The process or problem studied

- ❏ Key data collected

- ❏ Pivotal decisions made

- ❏ Mistakes, obstacles, and solutions

- ❏ Lessons learned and their impact

- ❏ Accomplishments and results

- ❏ Status at the time of completion

If your team maintained a team notebook, compiling a final report shouldn't be too difficult. You've already documented your original plan, midstream changes, learning experiences, problems, and solutions.

To prevent past problems from recurring, many teams develop and install a continuing control system before they disband. You're probably in the best position to build and start an early warning system. Also, if you can, turn your final report into training materials so your newfound expertise will not be lost.

The Final Presentation

Next, you should publicly announce successful completion of the project at a final presentation. Even though you've been debriefing your team sponsor right up to the end, the big picture often gets lost. Plan a final summary to close out the project. Invite senior management, involved stakeholders, and even external customers. You may get approval to take your show on the road to parade your accomplishments. Sometimes a final presentation gets turned into a training class for anyone who could benefit from what you learned.

Refer to earlier guidelines about effective presentations, and do this one right. You may not want to hire dancers and a band, but do prepare snazzy color visuals and provide refreshments. Hand out copies of your final report and broadly distribute it as a technical article.

Team Member Closure

This is the time to celebrate overall project completion and recognize all those who contributed. Make your final bash a celebration worthy of what you have achieved.

If this was your first high-performance team and your work was successful, you've undoubtedly experienced tremendous personal development. Seek out a new position where you can use what you learned. Now that you're an expert in the problem or process you studied, you could contribute as a trainer. Maybe you would like to be the nucleus of another unit that could profit from your expertise. Or maybe you're ready to be a team leader or facilitator. Talk to your boss about your career and next steps. And make sure that your contributions are included in your performance review.

Your final focus should be on the team's redeployment. You built a unit that's worked hard. Now your charter is complete and you are successful. It's time to disband the team and move on. But maybe you don't want to break up.

If you want to stay together, you could decide to extend your team charter. All you need to do is convince your team sponsor of the value of continuing. Or you could entirely redo your charter with a new challenge if you can gain management support.

PERSONAL ACTION PLAN

What are your priorities for working in a team?

_____
_____
_____

What main benefits do you think you will gain?

_____
_____
_____

What pitfalls do you especially want to avoid?

_____
_____
_____

What specifically do you want to share with your teammates?

_____
_____
_____

What are your plans for working in teams in the future?

_____
_____
_____

Now Available From

Books•Videos•CD-ROMs•Computer-Based Training Products

If you enjoyed this book, we have great news for you.
There are over 200 books available in the *Fifty-Minute™ Series*.
To request a free full-line catalog, contact your local distributor or

Crisp Learning
1200 Hamilton Court
Menlo Park, CA 94025
1-800-442-7477
CrispLearning.com

Subject Areas Include:

Management
Human Resources
Communication Skills
Personal Development
Marketing/Sales
Organizational Development
Customer Service/Quality
Computer Skills
Small Business and Entrepreneurship
Adult Literacy and Learning
Life Planning and Retirement

VERL

CRISP V ~~ORLDWIDE DISTRIBUTION~~ ION

728
London Life, London T-005
HR Training & Education
Working in teams
May 16, 2006

English language books are ~~available through~~ distributors include:

ASIA/PACIFIC

Australia/New Zealand: In Learning, PO Box 1051, Springwood QLD, Brisbane, Australia 4127   Tel: 61-7-3-841-2286, Facsimile: 61-7-3-841-1580
ATTN: Messrs. Richard/Robert Gordon

Hong Kong/Mainland China: Crisp Learning Solutions, 18/F Honest Motors Building 9-11 Leighton Rd., Causeway Bay, Hong Kong   Tel: 852-2915-7119,
Facsimile: 852-2865-2815 ATTN: Ms. Grace Lee

Indonesia: Pt Lutan Edukasi, Citra Graha, 7th Floor, Suite 701A, Jl. Jend. Gato Subroto Kav. 35-36, Jakarta 12950 Indonesia Tel: 62-21-527-9060/527-9061 Facsimile: 62-21-527-9062 ATTN: Mr. Suwardi Luis

Japan: Phoenix Associates, Believe Mita Bldg., 8th Floor 3-43-16 Shiba, Minato-ku, Tokyo 105-0014, Japan   Tel: 81-3-5427-6231, Facsimile: 81-3-5427-6232
ATTN: Mr. Peter Owans

Malaysia, Philippines, Singapore: Epsys Pte Ltd., 540 Sims Ave #04-01, Sims Avenue Centre, 387603, Singapore   Tel: 65-747-1964, Facsimile: 65-747-0162 ATTN: Mr. Jack Chin

CANADA

Crisp Learning Canada, 60 Briarwood Avenue, Mississauga, ON L5G 3N6 Canada
Tel: 905-274-5678, Facsimile: 905-278-2801 ATTN: Mr. Steve Connolly

EUROPEAN UNION

England: Flex Learning Media, Ltd., 9-15 Hitchin Street,
Baldock, Hertfordshire, SG7 6AL, England
Tel: 44-1-46-289-6000, Facsimile: 44-1-46-289-2417   ATTN: Mr. David Willetts

INDIA

Multi-Media HRD, Pvt. Ltd., National House, Floor 1, 6 Tulloch Road,
Appolo Bunder, Bombay, India 400-039 Tel: 91-22-204-2281,
Facsimile: 91-22-283-6478 ATTN: Messrs. Ajay Aggarwal/ C.L. Aggarwal

SOUTH AMERICA

Mexico: Grupo Editorial Iberoamerica, Nebraska 199, Col. Napoles, 03810 Mexico, D.F.
Tel: 525-523-0994, Facsimile: 525-543-1173   ATTN: Señor Nicholas Grepe

SOUTH AFRICA

Corporate: Learning Resources, PO Box 2806, Parklands, Johannesburg 2121, South Africa, Tel: 27-21-531-2923, Facsimile: 27-21-531-2944 ATTN: Mr. Ricky Robinson

MIDDLE EAST

Edutech Middle East, L.L.C., PO Box 52334, Dubai U.A.E.
Tel: 971-4-359-1222, Facsimile: 971-4-359-6500   ATTN: Mr. A.S.F. Karim